Curriculum Visions

Move on with
Fractions

Bria

Bass

Curriculum Visions

There's much more online including videos

You will find multimedia resources covering a wide range of topics at:

www.CurriculumVisions.com

CurriculumVisions is a subscription web site.

A CVP Book
Copyright © 2009 Atlantic Europe Publishing

Series Concept
Brian Knapp, BSc, PhD

Text contributed by
*Brian Knapp, BSc, PhD,
and Colin Bass, BSc, MA*

Editors
*Lorna Gilbert, Barbara Carragher,
and Gillian Gatehouse*

Senior Designer
Adele Humphries, BA, PGCE

Illustrations
David Woodroffe

Designed and produced by
Atlantic Europe Publishing

Printed in China by
WKT Company Ltd

Curriculum Visions Move on with Maths – Fractions
**A CIP record for this book is
available from the British Library**

ISBN: 978 1 86214 560 3

Picture credits
All photographs are from the Earthscape Picture Library and ShutterStock collections.

This product is manufactured from sustainable managed forests. For every tree cut down at least one more is planted.

Look out for these sections to help you learn more about each topic:

 Remember... This provides a summary of the key concept(s) on each two-page entry. Use it to revise what you have learned.

Can you do this? These problems reinforce the concepts learned on a particular spread, and can be used to test existing knowledge.

Answers to the problems set in the 'Move on with Maths' series can be found at: **www.curriculumvisions.com/moveOnAnswers**

Place value

To make it easy for you to see exactly what we are doing, you will find coloured columns behind the numbers in all the examples on this and the following pages. This is what the colours mean:

Ten thousands of units	Thousands of units	Hundreds of units	Tens of units	Units	Tenths of a unit	Hundredths of a unit	Thousandths of a unit
10,000	1,000	100	10	1	$\frac{1}{10}$	$\frac{1}{100}$	$\frac{1}{1,000}$

$$7 \ 1 \ 9 \ 6 \ 4 \ . \ 2 \ 3 \ 5$$

Whole numbers — Decimal point — Decimal parts

Contents

Finding out about fractions

A fraction is a share of something.

The most common shares are halves – when we split (divide) something into two equal parts – and quarters – when we split something into four equal parts.

Quarters are an important part of US currency.

1 or
One unit

$\frac{1}{2}$	$\frac{1}{2}$

Halves

$\frac{1}{4}$	$\frac{1}{4}$	$\frac{1}{4}$	$\frac{1}{4}$

Quarters

$\frac{1}{4}$	$\frac{3}{4}$

Quarters

Parts of a fraction

Fractions can be written in two ways. You will see them written in both ways throughout this book.

The number of parts we have
(also called numerator)

3/4

Dividing line

The number of parts
the original was split
into (also called
denominator)

The number of parts we have
(also called numerator)

Dividing line

$\dfrac{3}{4}$

The number
of parts the
original was split
into (also called
denominator)

Sharing the chocolate bar

Jilly had a chocolate bar. Like most chocolate bars, it was made into a number of blocks joined together.

She broke off (divided up) one of the four sections (fractions). This gave her a piece with three sections, and the fourth piece she was about to eat.

Because Jilly was eating a fourth of the bar, she was eating a quarter. A quarter, one-fourth, is written ¹/₄.

What remained behind was three-fourths (three-quarters), which is written as ³/₄.

Together the quarter section and the three-quarters section could be fitted together again to make a complete bar.

Can you do this? Jilly broke the chocolate bar in the picture into two halves, then broke one of the halves into half again. On a piece of paper, write in fractions (like those at the top of the page) the names of the shares she had before she ate any.

 Remember... Fractions are shares of a whole. The total number of shares is at the bottom of the fraction; the number of equal shares used is on the top.

Quarters of many shapes

You make fractions by dividing something into equal parts. Notice that shape does not affect the fraction because a fraction is simply a share of the whole; it tells us nothing about the real size or shape.

You can make fractions by breaking something like a bar of chocolate into equal pieces by size as we saw on page 5.

There are many other ways to make quarters. For example, you could split up a bag of sweets by weight using scales. You could also make fractions by volume, splitting a box of orange drink into equal amounts in several glasses. Here are some objects split up to show you the principle.

These two pieces of material have been cut into four equal pieces. Each is a quarter (¼) of the original.

$\frac{1}{4}$ $\frac{1}{4}$

$\frac{1}{4}$ $\frac{1}{4}$

$\frac{1}{4}$ $\frac{1}{4}$ $\frac{1}{4}$ $\frac{1}{4}$

This cake is divided into four equal sized fractions. To do this, the cut lines make a cross.

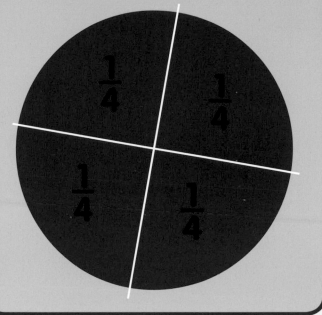

This is an equilateral triangle.

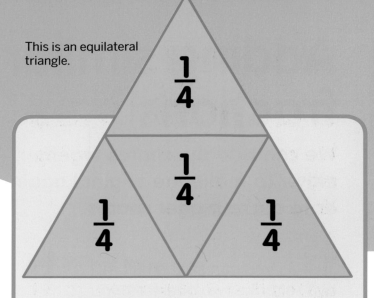

This triangle can be cut into four equal parts, each of which is also a triangle whose sides are all equal. Notice how they fit together.

Below you see four equal portions of orange drink. The words 'equal portion' are used to mean fraction in this case because the whole box was poured evenly into each glass so that all glasses contain the same share.

 Remember… Each of four equal parts is called one-quarter, not one-fourth. Each of two equal parts is called one-half, not one-second. All the other fractions are named using the sort of numbers we use for dates, such as one third, two fifths, thirteen twentieths, one thirtieth, four fifteenths, and so on.

Can you do this? On a separate piece of paper draw a picture showing a ball cut into four quarters.

Adding similar fractions

We can add the shares together, either to make the original again, or to make bigger shares.

Just as you can split a half in two to make two quarters, you can fit two quarters together to make a half.

Tempting chocolate

<u>Fractions can only be added if they share the same number at the bottom.</u> These kinds of fractions are called similar fractions.

Alfie was feeling particularly greedy because he liked chocolate a lot. So he broke off two quarters to eat.

He was going to eat two quarters or $^2/_4$. As you can see, this was also one half or $^1/_2$.

This was also exactly what was left: two quarters or one half.

In fact you can see that Alfie had taken two quarters to make a half.

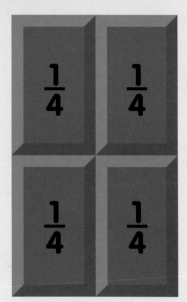

$$\frac{1}{4} + \frac{1}{4} = \frac{1}{2}$$

1 Start with a unit (**1**) and then write under it the number of pieces you are splitting (dividing) it into. So if you divide it into **4**, each piece is the unit (**1**) divided by **4**, hence ¼.

    If you have three of them, you have ³⁄₄, which you work out by adding the top numbers of the fractions together.

$$\frac{1}{4} + \frac{1}{4} + \frac{1}{4} = \frac{3}{4}$$

2 If you have four pieces, you have a whole bar (⁴⁄₄).

$$\frac{1}{4} + \frac{1}{4} + \frac{1}{4} + \frac{1}{4} = \frac{4}{4}$$

$$\frac{4}{4} = 1$$

See how these other fractions add up to 1¼

$$\frac{1}{4} + \frac{1}{4} + \frac{1}{4} + \frac{1}{4} + \frac{1}{4} = \frac{5}{4} = 1\frac{1}{4}$$

(See page 24 for more on improper fractions and mixed numbers.)

 Remember… You add similar fractions simply by adding the top numbers this way: ¹⁄₅ + ²⁄₅ = ³⁄₅ and ²⁄₇ + ³⁄₇ = ⁵⁄₇.

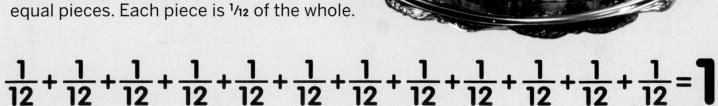

Here is a cake that has been cut into **12** equal pieces. Each piece is ¹⁄₁₂ of the whole.

$$\frac{1}{12} + \frac{1}{12} + \frac{1}{12} + \frac{1}{12} + \frac{1}{12} + \frac{1}{12} + \frac{1}{12} + \frac{1}{12} + \frac{1}{12} + \frac{1}{12} + \frac{1}{12} + \frac{1}{12} = 1$$

Can you do this? Can you think of a simpler name for ³⁄₁₂?

Multiplying fractions

Instead of adding fractions, sometimes it is easier to multiply a fraction by a whole number.

Each piece of this block of chocolate (**1** unit) is ¼ of the block.

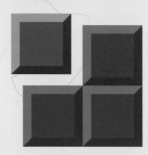

As one portion is $\dfrac{1}{4}$

Three portions are therefore $\dfrac{1}{4} + \dfrac{1}{4} + \dfrac{1}{4} = \dfrac{3}{4}$

But if we took any one of the three fractions (¼) and multiplied it by the number of fractions (**3**), we would get the same result, like this:

$$3 \times \dfrac{1}{4} = \dfrac{3}{4}$$

So multiplying is a quick way of adding.

To find four lots of two ninths (a quick way of finding ²⁄₉ + ²⁄₉ + ²⁄₉ + ²⁄₉).

Multiply the whole number (**4**) by the top of the fraction (**2**). This gives the fraction ⁸⁄₉.

Check your answer by adding the tops of the fractions: **2 + 2 + 2 + 2 = 8**.

$$4 \times \dfrac{2}{9} = \,?$$

Multiply the whole number **4** by the top of the fraction

$$\dfrac{4 \times 2}{9} = \dfrac{8}{9}$$

Here we are finding three lots of seven twenty-fifths (this is a quick way of finding $7/25 + 7/25 + 7/25$).

Multiply the whole number (**3**) by the top of the fraction (**7**). This gives the fraction $21/25$.

Check your answer by adding the tops of the fractions: **7 + 7 + 7 = 21**.

$$3 \times \frac{7}{25} = ?$$

Multiply the whole number **3** by the top of the fraction

$$\frac{3 \times 7}{25} = \frac{21}{25}$$

Emma was planning how to run a cross country race. She intended to use the first quarter mile to place herself about in the middle of the other runners. Then for **1¾** miles she would just keep pace with them. For the next **1½** miles she hoped to increase the pace and move near the front. Then for **1¼** mile she would run gently conserving her breath but not falling back. That should leave her well placed and with enough puff for a strong finish to overtake any challengers in the last **¾** mile. How long was the race?

We have to add up **¼ + 1¾ + 1½ + 1¼ + ¾**.

As the smallest fractions involved are quarters, we must turn all the numbers into quarters, like this.

$1/4 + 7/4 + 6/4 + 5/4 + 3/4$.

Now we can add all the top numbers:

1 + 7 + 6 + 5 + 3 = 22.

So the race was **22** quarters of a mile, or $22/4$.

Finally we do the short division to turn this into whole miles and a fraction.

$$4\overline{)2\ 2}$$
$$5 \text{ rem } 2$$

So that is **5 + $2/4$ or 5½ miles**.

⟫⟫ **Remember…** When we multiply fractions by whole numbers, we multiply the top of the fraction by the whole number.

Can you do these? $3 \times 2/12 = ?$

$2 \times 5/12 = ?$

Work the answers out on a separate piece of paper.

Smaller and smaller fractions

An easy way to divide something is to halve it, and then halve it again and again.

Halving gives you portions that have numbers like **2**, **4**, **8**, **16**, **32** and so on. You simply cut in half again and again until you have the number of fractions you want.

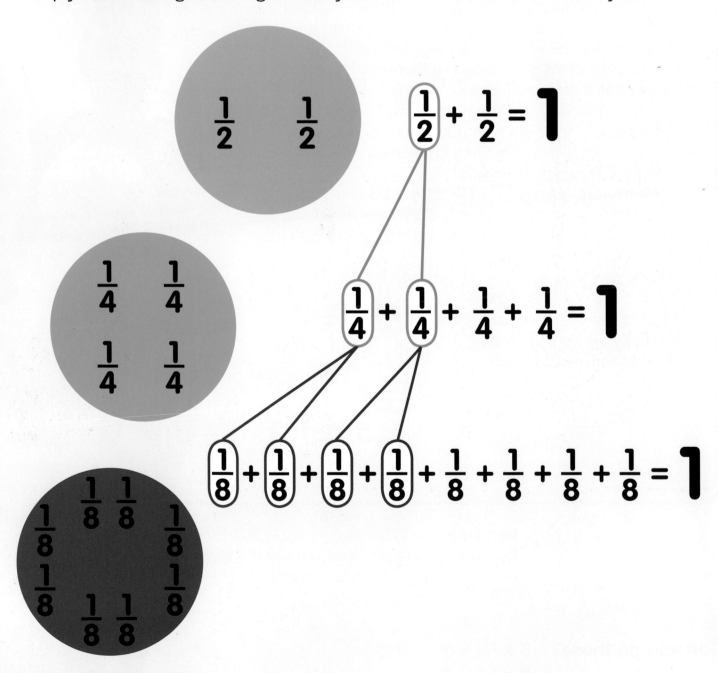

$$\frac{1}{2} + \frac{1}{2} = 1$$

$$\frac{1}{4} + \frac{1}{4} + \frac{1}{4} + \frac{1}{4} = 1$$

$$\frac{1}{8} + \frac{1}{8} + \frac{1}{8} + \frac{1}{8} + \frac{1}{8} + \frac{1}{8} + \frac{1}{8} + \frac{1}{8} = 1$$

The birthday cake

Sammy was having a birthday party, and so a huge cake was baked for the occasion. There were to be **15** guests, and each of them needed to have an equal share of the cake. Nobody could think how to cut the cake into **15** equal portions, but then Sammy had a bright idea – cut the cake into **16** and then keep one piece back so that he could have it tomorrow.

So at the party they cut the cake across (making **2** portions), then across again (making **4**). Then they cut each quarter to make **8** (see page 12) and then cut each eighth to make **16** portions.

But just as Sammy was about to put the spare piece away, another friend turned up by surprise. So the extra piece came in handy after all!

$$\frac{1}{16} + \frac{1}{16} + \frac{1}{16} + \frac{1}{16} + \frac{1}{16} + \frac{1}{16} + \frac{1}{16} + \frac{1}{16} + \frac{1}{16} + \frac{1}{16} + \frac{1}{16} + \frac{1}{16} + \frac{1}{16} + \frac{1}{16} + \frac{1}{16} + \frac{1}{16} = 1$$

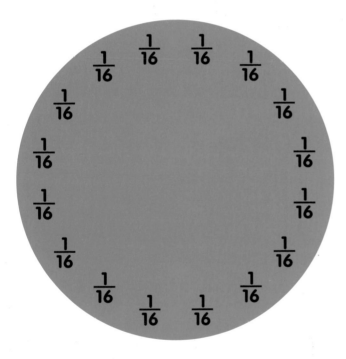

 Remember... Every time we share a piece by cutting it in two, each piece gets smaller, so we <u>multiply the bottom of each fraction by two</u>.

Can you do this?

On a separate piece of paper write half of $\frac{1}{32}$ as a fraction.

13

Mixing and matching

When you have fractions that are not similar, multiply one group up so that all fractions become the same at the bottom.

A not-so-quiet meal

Gill was going to give her two children a snack. So she got a pizza out of the freezer and reheated it in her microwave. Then, as there were just two of them, Gill divided the hot pizza into two equal portions, so that each child had a half each. So, $1 = \frac{2}{2}$.

$$1 = \frac{1}{2} + \frac{1}{2}$$

Just as she was about to put the pizza on the plates, the doorbell rang and two of the children's friends were standing there. Not wishing to be rude, Gill asked them if they would like a pizza snack. So, **1 = ⁴/₄**.

Now the four children had a quarter each.

$$1 = \frac{1}{4} + \frac{1}{4} + \frac{1}{4} + \frac{1}{4}$$

Then four more children arrived, so there were eight people to feed. So she microwaved another pizza.
2 = ⁴/₄ + ⁴/₄.

$$2 = \frac{1}{4} + \frac{1}{4} + \frac{1}{4} + \frac{1}{4}$$
$$+ \frac{1}{4} + \frac{1}{4} + \frac{1}{4} + \frac{1}{4}$$

However, although the first pizza had pepperoni topping, the second one had cheese topping. So Gill divided each pizza into **8** and gave a piece of each topping to everyone.

Pepperoni topping

$\frac{1}{8}$ $\frac{1}{8}$ $\frac{1}{8}$ $\frac{1}{8}$ $\frac{1}{8}$ $\frac{1}{8}$ $\frac{1}{8}$ $\frac{1}{8}$

Cheese topping

$\frac{1}{8}$ $\frac{1}{8}$ $\frac{1}{8}$ $\frac{1}{8}$ $\frac{1}{8}$ $\frac{1}{8}$ $\frac{1}{8}$ $\frac{1}{8}$

Each plate then had ⅛ cheese + ⅛ pepperoni. As there were two pizzas, each person got ¼ of a pizza:

$$\frac{1}{8} + \frac{1}{8} = \frac{2}{8} = \frac{1}{4}$$

Can you do this in your head?
How long is one quarter of two hours?

>>> **Remember...** One eighth of two is the same as one quarter of one. ²/₈ and ¼ have the same value. The diagrams show this clearly. They are called equivalent fractions.

Fractions with the same value

Fractions often look different from one another, but they can easily be made to look the same. Here's how.

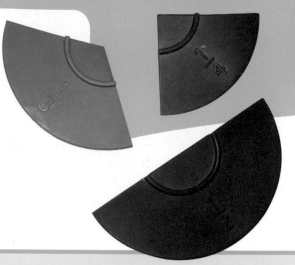

Halves, quarters and thirds are all different kinds of fraction because the bottom number, or denominator, is different.

When you have different fractions, it isn't always easy to know when one fraction is bigger than another. For example, which is the bigger of $2/3$ and $3/4$?

It is even harder to know which is the bigger of $7/9$ and $4/5$, for example.

To get around this problem we need to make the fractions the same kind. We do this by making the bottom numbers all the same. Then they become similar fractions.

$$\frac{1}{2}$$ This kind of fraction is based on **2**. Other fractions of a similar kind are $2/2$ and $3/2$.

$$\frac{1}{3}$$ This kind of fraction is based on **3**. Other fractions of a similar kind are $2/3$ and $3/3$.

$$\frac{1}{4}$$ This kind of fraction is based on **4**. Other fractions of a similar kind are $2/4$ and $3/4$.

Making fractions with the same value

Here are some examples of how we get some different-looking fractions with the same value as $1/4$:

Multiply the top and bottom by **2** to get $2/8$

Multiply the top and bottom by **6** to get $6/24$

$$\frac{1}{4} = \frac{2}{8} = \frac{6}{24}$$

Now look at the fractions which have the same value as $12/36$:

As you can see, many different-looking fractions are really fractions with the same value in disguise.

Divide the top and bottom by **2** to get $6/18$

Divide the top and bottom by **4** to get $3/9$

Divide the top and bottom by **12** to get $1/3$

$$\frac{12}{36} = \frac{6}{18} = \frac{3}{9} = \frac{1}{3}$$

Making similar fractions

This is done by changing the way we write one or both fractions until they are the same kind of fraction. To do this, we have to make the bottom numbers the same.

Of course, we must not change the value of the fraction. We keep it the same by multiplying the number on top of the fraction, the numerator, by the same number that we multiply the bottom.

For example, if we want to find out which is the bigger number, $^4/_5$ or $^7/_9$, we need to make them the same kind of fraction.

Is $\dfrac{4}{5}$ bigger than $\dfrac{7}{9}$?

1 Multiply the top and bottom of $^7/_9$ by **5**:

$$\frac{7}{9} = \frac{7 \times 5}{9 \times 5} = \frac{35}{45}$$

2 Multiply top and bottom of $^4/_5$ by **9**:

$$\frac{4}{5} = \frac{4 \times 9}{5 \times 9} = \frac{36}{45}$$

3 Now the fractions are the same kind because the bottom numbers are the same. But because we multiplied each fraction by the same number top and bottom, their values remained the same.

Now it is easy to see that $^{36}/_{45}$ is bigger than $^{35}/_{45}$, so $^4/_5$ is bigger than $^7/_9$.

$$\frac{36}{45} > \frac{35}{45} \text{ so therefore } \frac{4}{5} > \frac{7}{9}$$

>>>> **Remember...** Did you spot how we knew which numbers to multiply by? We used the bottom number of the other fraction. Just check back above to see how it was done.

Can you do this? Which is the bigger of $^{11}/_{18}$ and $^3/_5$?

Give your working out on a separate piece of paper.

Fractions that look different

Fractions that have the same value, even if they look different, are known as equivalent fractions.

Plum picking

Ian had been picking plums. He arranged the plums in rows so they were easier to count. Each row had **9** plums, and he had **6** rows. So the total was **9 × 6 = 54**.

He wanted to sell them in **18s**. He separated out **2** of the **6** rows (to make **18** plums), so the top two rows made a collection that was $^2/_6$ of the total.

Then he separated out another two rows. Now he had another collection that was $^2/_6$ of the total and what was left was also $^2/_6$ of the total.

There were **3** groups, so each group must also be one-third of the whole collection, or $^1/_3$.

There were **18** plums. So each group contained $^{18}/_{54}$ of the total. So this, too, was the equivalent of $^1/_3$ and these fractions all have the same value. They are equivalent fractions.

$$9 \times 6 = 54$$

$$\overset{18 \div 9}{\frac{18}{54}} \text{ or } \overset{2 \div 2}{\frac{2}{6}} \text{ or } \frac{1}{3}$$
$$\underset{54 \div 9}{\phantom{\frac{18}{54}}} \quad \underset{6 \div 2}{\phantom{\frac{2}{6}}}$$

$$\frac{18}{54} \text{ or } \frac{2}{6} \text{ or } \frac{1}{3}$$

$$\frac{18}{54} \text{ or } \frac{2}{6} \text{ or } \frac{1}{3}$$

Adele's class had been told that they would do Music for the first ¾ of the term, and Art for the last ⅔ of it. This was to make time for extra Hockey at the beginning of term, and time for Christmas preparations at the end. It was not rocket science to see that they would do both Art and Music for a good time in the middle of term because ¾ + ⅔ is more than one whole term. Adele was disappointed that they would do less Art than Music. Brad said she was wrong. There would be more Art, because ⅔ is bigger than ¾. Who was correct? For what fraction of the term did they do both?

We have to find equivalent fractions for ⅔ and for ¾ with the same denominator. Multiply top and bottom first by **2**, then by **3**, then by **4** until you find the answer.

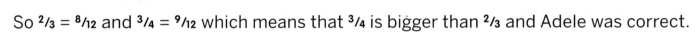

$$\frac{2}{3} = \frac{4}{6} = \frac{6}{9} = \frac{8}{12} = \frac{10}{15}$$

$$\frac{3}{4} = \frac{6}{8} = \frac{9}{12} = \frac{12}{16}$$

So ⅔ = ⁸⁄₁₂ and ¾ = ⁹⁄₁₂ which means that ¾ is bigger than ⅔ and Adele was correct.

Notice that we could have used the same method as on page 17 for making similar fractions.
⅔ × ⁴⁄₄ = ⁸⁄₁₂ and ¾ × ³⁄₃ = ⁹⁄₁₂. That is why the method on page 17 works.

$$\frac{2}{3} = \frac{2 \times 4}{3 \times 4} = \frac{8}{12}$$

$$\frac{3}{4} = \frac{3 \times 3}{4 \times 3} = \frac{9}{12}$$

If the term was **12** weeks long, they would do Music for the first **9** weeks, and Art for the last **8** weeks. That means **1** week less Art. One week is ¹⁄₁₂ of the term, and ⁹⁄₁₂ − ⁸⁄₁₂ = ¹⁄₁₂.

There would be **4** weeks at the beginning of term when they did not do Art, and **3** weeks at the end when they did not do Music. So there would be **4 + 3 = 7** weeks when they did NOT do both. That leaves **12 − 7 = 5** weeks in which they DID do both.

Can you do this? Which is the bigger of ⅓ and ⅜?

Give your working out on a separate piece of paper.
(You could check by dividing up a 24 hour day.)

 Remember... Fractions that look different sometimes have the same value. To find out, try to simplify the fraction by dividing top and bottom by the same number.

Adding unlike fractions

If you have two fractions to add, and their bottom numbers (denominators) are different, you will need to make them the same kind, or similar fractions.

½ + ⅓ cannot be added until the bottom numbers are the same.

1 Multiply the bottom of the fractions together **2 × 3 = 6**. This number can be used at the bottom of both fractions and is called the common denominator. In this case **6** is the common denominator.

$$\frac{1}{2} + \frac{1}{3} = \textbf{?}$$

2 Multiply the top and bottom of each fraction (as we did on page 16) to make the bottom **6**. This will keep the values the same as the original fractions.

3 Multiplying the top and bottom of ½ by **3** makes:

$$\frac{1 \times 3}{2 \times 3} = \frac{3}{6}$$

4 Multiplying the top and bottom of ⅓ by **2** makes:

$$\frac{1 \times 2}{3 \times 2} = \frac{2}{6}$$

5 Now you can add the top numbers, **3** and **2**.

$$\frac{3}{6} + \frac{2}{6} = \frac{5}{6}$$

The common denominator

 Remember... If you have two different-looking fractions and want to add them, make the bottoms the same kind.

How Flash Jimmy added unlike fractions to work out his wealth

SW, the head of the Sloshing Oil dynasty was fed up. He could not get anyone to marry his four daughters. Finally, he declared that he would divide up his wealth equally between the men who married his daughters.

Jimmy the slick salesman married the eldest daughter, Ermintrude, and collected one-quarter (¼) of SW's wealth. But no one would marry any of his other daughters, so ¾ of his wealth remained.

In desperation, SW offered to split the ¾ equally between each husband and the person who found his daughters a husband. So, ¾ split **6** ways = ³/₂₄ = ¹/₈.

Quick as a flash, Jimmy came back with three of his friends to marry the remaining daughters. Now Jimmy was richer by ¼ + ³/₈ of SW's wealth.

How much was that?

This is how he worked it out.

He knew they were different kinds of fraction so his task was to make them the same kind.

So he tried multiplying the top and bottom of ¼ by **2**:

$$\frac{1}{4} = \frac{1 \times 2}{4 \times 2} = \frac{2}{8}$$

So:

$$\frac{1}{4} + \frac{3}{8} \text{ is the same as } \frac{2}{8} + \frac{3}{8}$$

Both fractions had an **8** at the bottom, so they were similar fractions.

So the answer was:

$$\frac{2}{8} + \frac{3}{8} = \frac{5}{8}$$

Notice... Because, in this case, one bottom number divides into the other (**4** divides into **8**), we only have to multiply one fraction.

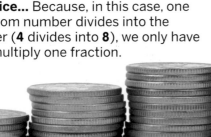

Can you do these?   ¹/₃ + ¼ = ?

⁵/₁₆ + ¹/₈ = ?   Work the answers out on a separate piece of paper.

21

Subtracting fractions

Subtracting fractions is also possible once the fractions have been made the same kind, that is, once you have made the bottom numbers the same.

1 Suppose we want to take ¼ from ½. In this case one fraction has the number **2** at the bottom, and the other has **4** at the bottom. We need to change these to be the same.

$$\frac{1}{2} - \frac{1}{4} = \textbf{?}$$

2 Here we multiply the bottom and also the top of the first fraction (½) by **2** to make it the equivalent fraction ²/₄.

$$\frac{1}{2} = \frac{2 \times 1}{2 \times 2} = \frac{2}{4}$$

3 Now it is easy; we simply subtract the top numbers, and the answer is ¼.

$$\frac{2}{4} - \frac{1}{4} = \frac{1}{4}$$

Jordan's mum had only ¾ pint of milk left for the weekend. She was worried whether it was enough. Jordan came down late for breakfast and put ⅓ pint on his muesli. How much milk was left now?

First make similar fractions.

$$\frac{3}{4} = \frac{3}{4} \times \frac{3}{3} = \frac{9}{12}$$

$$\frac{1}{3} = \frac{1}{3} \times \frac{4}{4} = \frac{4}{12}$$

Now $\quad \dfrac{3}{4} - \dfrac{1}{3} = \dfrac{9}{12} - \dfrac{4}{12} = \dfrac{5}{12}$

Jordan was sent shopping.

Enough flowers?

Stephanie was helping her aunt at the flower shop. They have **900** flowers in the shop. They had to supply a third (⅓) of their stock to a wedding and half (½) of it to a hotel at the end of the day. But they also had to supply customers waiting in the shop.

They found out how many flowers they could sell in the shop using fractions like this:

1

The wedding needed ⅓, and the hotel needed ½. Their total stock (**1**) in fractions was ¹⁄₁.

So what was left to sell was ¹⁄₁ − ⅓ − ½.

To find what fraction was left to sell they had to make the fractions the same kind. They did this by changing them all into sixths, which looks like this:

$$\frac{1}{1} - \frac{1}{3} - \frac{1}{2} = \textbf{?}$$

Multiply top and bottom by **6** Multiply top and bottom by **2** Multiply top and bottom by **3**

$$= \frac{6}{6} - \frac{2}{6} - \frac{3}{6}$$

For an explanation of why **6** was used as the bottom number on all the fractions, see page 20.

2

Now it is easy to subtract.

To give the answer:

$$= \frac{6 - 2 - 3}{6}$$

$$= \frac{1}{6}$$

3

So they could sell ⅙ of the stock of **900** flowers in the shop.

They worked out ⅙ of **900** by short division and found the answer to be **150**.

Provided they did not sell more than **150** before the end of the day, there would be no problem.

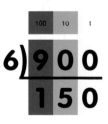

Can you do these?   ⅓ − ¼ = **?**

                        ⁵⁄₁₆ − ⅛ = **?**

Work the answers out on a separate piece of paper.

>>>> **Remember...** If you want to subtract fractions, then, just like adding, you first have to make the bottoms of each fraction the same number.

Fractions bigger than one

Top-heavy fractions, with the top number bigger than the bottom, tell you that you have more than a whole unit.

When we add fractions together, we can sometimes end up with more than a whole unit (for example, $^5/_4$, when a whole unit is $^4/_4$).
 If we write these 'top-heavy' fractions – called improper fractions – as whole numbers and fractions, they are called mixed numbers.

$$\frac{5}{4} = \frac{1}{4} + \frac{1}{4} + \frac{1}{4} + \frac{1}{4} + \frac{1}{4} = 1\frac{1}{4}$$

Improper fraction   Mixed number

The (shorter) International motor racing circuit at Silverstone is **2¼ miles** long. How far is **5** laps of it?
 Five laps can be worked out either by:

$$2 + \frac{1}{4} + 2 + \frac{1}{4} + 2 + \frac{1}{4} + 2 + \frac{1}{4} + 2 + \frac{1}{4} \quad \textbf{OR}$$

$$2 + 2 + 2 + 2 + 2 + \frac{1}{4} + \frac{1}{4} + \frac{1}{4} + \frac{1}{4} + \frac{1}{4}$$

$$= 10 + \frac{5}{4} = 10 + 1\frac{1}{4} = 11\frac{1}{4}$$

Or more easily by $2\frac{1}{4} \times 5 = 2 \times 5 + \frac{1}{4} \times 5 = 10 + \frac{5}{4} = 10 + 1\frac{1}{4} = 11\frac{1}{4}$ **miles**.
 The second method would definitely be easier to work out the total length of **55** laps.

 Remember… Improper fractions are simply ordinary fractions with a value bigger than **1**.

Lots left over

When Cherie's party was over, pieces of two cakes and two apple pies remained on the table.

Portions had been eaten from both of the cakes and apple pies. How much of each kind was left?

Cherry cake

To add the two pieces of cherry cake.

$$\frac{1}{2} + \frac{7}{8}$$

Apple pies

To add the two pieces of apple pie.

$$\frac{2}{3} + \frac{3}{8}$$

1 Make the bottoms the same.

$$\underset{2 \times 4}{\overset{1 \times 4}{\frac{4}{8}}} + \frac{7}{8}$$

Make the bottoms the same.

$$= \underset{3 \times 8}{\overset{2 \times 8}{\frac{16}{24}}} + \underset{8 \times 3}{\overset{3 \times 3}{\frac{9}{24}}}$$

2 Add them. $\quad = \dfrac{11}{8}$

Add them. $\quad = \dfrac{25}{24}$

3 Separate any whole numbers.

$$= \frac{8}{8} + \frac{3}{8}$$

Separate any whole numbers.

$$= \frac{24}{24} + \frac{1}{24}$$

4 Write the answer as a whole number and a fraction side by side.

$$= 1\frac{3}{8}$$

Write the answer as a whole number and a fraction side by side.

$$= 1\frac{1}{24}$$

Can you do these? $\quad ^3/_4 + ^3/_8 = ?$

$^7/_{12} + ^5/_8 = ?$ Work the answers out on a separate piece of paper.

Adding mixed numbers

Adding mixed numbers is easiest once you have separated out the whole numbers and given all the fractions the same bottom numbers.

Changing top-heavy fractions into mixed numbers

If we have top-heavy fractions such as: $\dfrac{10}{3} + \dfrac{27}{6} = \mathbf{?}$

1 Turn the top-heavy fractions into mixed numbers, and then separate out the whole numbers:

$$\frac{10}{3} + \frac{27}{6} = \mathbf{?}$$

$$\frac{10}{3} = 3\frac{1}{3} = 3 + \frac{1}{3} \qquad \frac{27}{6} = 4\frac{3}{6} = 4 + \frac{3}{6}$$

So, the calculation for $^{10}/_3 + {}^{27}/_6$ is now:

$$3 + \frac{1}{3} + 4 + \frac{3}{6}$$

2 Add the whole numbers:

$$7 + \frac{1}{3} + \frac{3}{6}$$

3 Convert the fractions so they have the same bottoms ($^1/_3 = {}^2/_6$):

$$7 + \frac{2}{6} + \frac{3}{6}$$

4 Add the whole numbers and the fractions:

$$7 + \frac{5}{6} = 7\frac{5}{6}$$

Adding mixed numbers

Adding mixed numbers is straightforward. Take the calculation:

$$2\tfrac{1}{2} + 1\tfrac{7}{8} = \;?$$

1 Separate out the whole numbers and fractions:

$$= 2 + \tfrac{1}{2} + 1 + \tfrac{7}{8}$$

2 Add the whole numbers:

$$= 3 + \tfrac{1}{2} + \tfrac{7}{8}$$

3 Make the bottoms of the fractions the same ($\tfrac{1}{2} = \tfrac{4}{8}$):

$$= 3 + \tfrac{4}{8} + \tfrac{7}{8}$$

4 Add the fractions:

$$= 3 + \tfrac{11}{8}$$

5 Turn the top-heavy fraction into a mixed number ($\tfrac{11}{8} = 1 + \tfrac{3}{8}$):

$$= 3 + 1 + \tfrac{3}{8}$$

6 Add to the whole numbers:

$$= 4\tfrac{3}{8}$$

 Remember... It is easier to add and subtract whole numbers than fractions, so keep to whole numbers as much as you can.

Can you do these? $\tfrac{7}{4} + \tfrac{11}{8} = \;?$

$$3\tfrac{3}{4} + 1\tfrac{5}{6} = \;?$$

Work the answers out on a separate piece of paper.

Subtracting mixed numbers

If you have mixed numbers separate the whole numbers from the fractions first.

Subtracting the mixed numbers

Graham and Fi wanted to make a drink containing orange juice. They had **3³/₈** bottles of juice. It would need **1¹/₂** bottles of juice to make the drink. How much was left at the end?
They needed to work out:

$$3\tfrac{3}{8} - 1\tfrac{1}{2} = ?$$

1 Make all the bottoms of the fractions the same (change ¹/₂ to ⁴/₈):

$$= 3 + \tfrac{3}{8} - 1 - \tfrac{4}{8}$$

2 Because ⁴/₈ is too big to be taken from ³/₈, we borrow one of the three whole numbers and write it as ⁸/₈:

$$= 2 + \tfrac{8}{8} + \tfrac{3}{8} - 1 - \tfrac{4}{8}$$

3 Subtract the whole numbers (**2 – 1 = 1**):

$$= 1 + \tfrac{8}{8} + \tfrac{3}{8} - \tfrac{4}{8}$$

4 Now work out the fraction:
⁸/₈ + ³/₈ = ¹¹/₈
¹¹/₈ – ⁴/₈ = ⁷/₈

$$= 1 + \frac{8 + 3 - 4}{8}$$

The answer is:

$$= 1 + \tfrac{7}{8} \quad = 1\tfrac{7}{8}$$

Jamie and Katie were having a **12 lengths** swimming race. When Jamie had swum **5¾ lengths**, Katie had already swum **8½ lengths**. How far ahead was Katie at this stage?

We have to work out **8½ − 5¾**, which is **8²/₄ − 5³/₄**. Splitting up the whole numbers and fractions gives

$$8 - 5 + \frac{2}{4} - \frac{3}{4}$$

$$= 3 + \frac{2}{4} - \frac{3}{4}$$

As ³/₄ is bigger than ²/₄, we borrow a unit:

$$= 2 + \frac{4}{4} + \frac{2}{4} - \frac{3}{4}$$

$$= 2 + \frac{3}{4}$$

Katie was **2¾** lengths ahead.

Remember... It is easier to work with mixed numbers than with improper fractions, so convert improper fractions whenever you can.

Can you do these?   ⁷/₄ − ¹¹/₈ = ?

3³/₄ − 1⁵/₆ = ?

Work the answers out on a separate piece of paper.

Ratio and proportion

A ratio compares different numbers of the same thing, while proportion compares numbers of different kinds of thing.

Suppose we wanted to talk about the steepness of a slope. In this case we would be comparing how far you go along to how far you go up. So we are comparing like things (in this case lengths).

In many cases the ratio is disguised by the word "in". So, a slope with a steepness of **1 in 2** is a slope where you go **1** up or down for each **2** you go along.

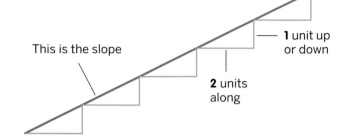

This is the slope

1 unit up or down

2 units along

This can be written down as a ratio **1:2**.

Suppose we wanted to hire a car for a few days.

If hiring it cost **£25** a day, the total costs would be in proportion to the number of days.

Days	1	2	3	4
Cost (£)	25	50	75	100

Clare's Mum is thinking of joining the local Spa Club.
She has been sent the membership costs.

Membership Type	Joining Fee	Monthly payment	Number of Visits a year
Full	£99.00	£28.00	12
Club 3	£99.00	£9.00	3
Club 6	£99.00	£18.00	6

Club 3 and Club 6, like Full membership, allow you to go any time of the day or week.
Six visits a year seems to cost twice as much as three visits a year.
6:3 is a ratio of **2:1**, and **£18:£9** is also a ratio of **2:1**.
The costs appear to be in proportion to the number of visits.
But they are not, because of the Joining Fee.
You have to join for a whole year, so Club 3 costs **£9 × 12 + £99 = £108 + £99 = £207** for a year.
Club 6 costs **£18 × 12 + £99 = £216 + £99 = £315** for a year.
The ratio of costs is **315:207** which is **315/207:1** or **1.52:1**. This is cheaper than **2:1**.
Perhaps Full membership would be better still?
It would cost **£28 × 12 + £99 = £336 + £99 = £435** for a year.
Compared with Club 3, the number of visits allowed is a ratio of **12:3 = 4:1**.
The ratio of costs is only **435:207 = 2.10:1**.
Putting it another way, if the costs were in proportion to the number of visits, they would be:

Number of visits	Cost for a year
3	207
6	414
12	828

But Clare's Mum did not know whether she would want to visit as much as twelve times a year.

 Remember... Ratios are similar to fractions. They are used to compare similar things, like the steepness of a slope, the number of gear teeth or diameters.

Can you do these – ratio or proportion?
On your bike, which would you use to compare the number of times you turn the pedals to the number of times the back wheel goes round?
On your bike, which would you use to compare the number of times you turn the pedals to the distance you go forward?

Write your answers on a separate piece of paper.

More on proportion

We use proportion to compare the numbers in different collections of things. The numbers in each collection are usually different kinds of things.

Gran's summer drink recipe

Jenny and Pete were confused. They were getting ready for some friends to arrive that afternoon. They were staying in Canada, where people use metric measures, but their Gran lived in the United States, where they use US measures. She had sent them a recipe for a refreshing cool drink for summer days.

RECIPE CLIPPINGS

Gran's Grapefruit Guzzler

1. Put 1 fl oz of concentrated grapefruit juice in a jug.

2. Add 1 cup of lemonade.

3. Add a pint of fresh cold water.

Stir it up, add ice cubes, and leave it to stand in a cool shady place until all the ice has melted.

Then serve immediately.

The only jug they had was a 1-litre jug. How could they measure a pint of water in a litre jug? How big a cup should they use? What is a 'fl oz'?

They went on line to look it up. They found these results.

US Measure

8 fl oz (fluid ounces) = 1 cup = $\frac{1}{2}$ pt

16 fl oz = 2 cups = 1 pint

Clear

Using proportion

First they needed to change everything into the same kind of measure. They chose to use US fluid ounces.

These are the fluid ounces of the ingredients:

Grapefruit concentrate		=	**1 fl oz**
Lemonade	**1 cup**	=	**8 fl oz**
Water	**1 pint**	=	**16 fl oz**

Grapefruit concentrate 1 : Lemonade 8 : Water 16

This seemed a hard problem. But in fact they didn't even need a calculator or a pint jug or even a litre jug. They still didn't have anything that measured fluid ounces. This is where proportion came in. Once they knew the ratios of the ingredients they could forget all about fluid ounces.

They used a big container and one of their own glasses to measure out the ingredients in the same proportion as Gran's recipe into a big bowl: **1** glass of juice, **8** glasses of lemonade, **16** glasses of water.

So they had **1 + 8 + 16 = 25** glasses of drink.

Now they could see how to make **50** glasses of drink by increasing everything proportionally by **2**, or whatever proportion they wanted.

Grapefruit concentrate 2 : Lemonade 16 : Water 32

 Remember... All the ratios had to be in the same units before the drinks could be mixed in proportional amounts.

Per cent

Percentage, %, means 'for each hundred'. Percentages are a quick way of comparing sizes.

Percentages are numbers like the tops of fractions in which the bottom numbers have all already been fixed as **100**. This makes them very easy to compare.
   Mathematicians use a special symbol, % to mean per cent or '/100'.

To make a fraction into a percentage, all we do is multiply the top (numerator) by **100** and then divide by the bottom (denominator) and add a % sign.

$$\text{Percentage} = \frac{\text{Numerator}}{\text{Denominator}} \times 100\%$$

Convert ¼ into a percentage:

1 Multiply **1** (the top) by **100**:

$$\frac{1}{4} \times 100 = \frac{100}{4}$$

2 Divide by **4** (the bottom), then add the % (per cent) sign:

$$= 25\%$$

Here are some common fractions written as percentages.

½ as a percentage:

$$\frac{1}{2} \times 100 = \frac{100}{2} = 50\%$$

¾ as a percentage:

$$\frac{3}{4} \times 100 = \frac{300}{4} = 75\%$$

⅝ as a percentage:

$$\frac{5}{8} \times 100 = \frac{500}{8} = 62\frac{1}{2}\%$$

⅓ as a percentage:

$$\frac{1}{3} \times 100 = \frac{100}{3} = 33\frac{1}{3}\%$$

⅔ as a percentage:

$$\frac{2}{3} \times 100 = \frac{200}{3} = 66\frac{2}{3}\%$$

Can you do these?
On a separate piece of
paper, write as percentages:

$\frac{1}{10}$

$\frac{3}{20}$

$\frac{1}{100}$

>>> **Remember...** Some calculators
have a per cent key. Press **1**, then
÷, then **3**, then **%** to check the
percentage equal to ⅓ (**33.3%**).

Percentages as fractions

Here is how to convert between fractions and percentages.

To turn a percentage into a fraction

To turn a percentage into a fraction, divide it by **100**, and then reduce it to the simplest possible fraction.

The top and bottom can be divided by **10**, so $^{10}/_{100}$ simplifies to $^1/_{10}$.

$$10\% = \frac{10}{100} = \frac{1}{10}$$

To turn **20%** into a fraction, divide by **100**, then simplify by division:

$$20\% = \underset{100 \div 10}{\overset{20 \div 10}{\frac{20}{100}}} = \underset{10 \div 2}{\overset{2 \div 2}{\frac{2}{10}}} = \frac{1}{5}$$

To turn **60%** into a fraction, divide by **100**, then simplify by division:

$$60\% = \underset{100 \div 10}{\overset{60 \div 10}{\frac{60}{100}}} = \underset{10 \div 2}{\overset{6 \div 2}{\frac{6}{10}}} = \frac{3}{5}$$

Sometimes you can't reduce it at all, such as in the case of **63%**:

$$63\% = \frac{63}{100}$$

And then you simply have to leave it as it is.

Jason wanted to compare how successful England, Australia and New Zealand are at Rugby Union internationals. The problem was they had not played the same number of games. These were the results he found.

TEAM	PLAYED	WON	LOST	DRAWN
England	609	324	237	48
Australia	459	238	207	14
New Zealand	443	328	96	19

Obviously New Zealand are the most successful, as they have won more games than the others, even though they have played fewest. But how much better are they?

Jason worked out their winning percentages using a calculator.

England: $324 \div 609 \times 100 = 53.20\%$
Australia: $238 \div 459 \times 100 = 51.85\%$
New Zealand: $328 \div 443 \times 100 = 74.04\%$

So against all international opposition (not only each other) out of every hundred games played, Australia have won just over a half of them, England have done about the same, winning about **1½** more matches in every hundred played (or **3** in **200**) while New Zealand have won nearly three quarters of their matches (**3** games out of every **4**).

Can you do this? Use a calculator to work out the percentage of games each nation lost in the table above.

Give your answers on a separate piece of paper.

 Remember... Percentages are often widely used instead of fractions. To convert to a fraction, just divide the percentage by **100**.

Per cent more

Percentage more means the extra percentage added to the original.

You often see signs on the items in shops saying that you are offered so much per cent more. Here is an example:

25% of the original amount added

25% of the original amount

The original amount

25% EXTRA FREE

SCRUNCHY FLAKES

25% extra free on your cornflakes

The new amount is the original amount of cornflakes **+ 25% of the original**, **25%** more means an extra ¼.

$$25\% = \frac{1}{4}$$

$$100\% = \frac{4}{4}$$

That is, for every four cornflakes you pay for, you get one more free.

$$\frac{1}{4} + \frac{4}{4} = \frac{5}{4} = \mathbf{125\%}$$

Lucky Jim

Here is an example of 'per cent more' with a twist. See how we can use the fraction to find out what discount we have been given.

Jim went to buy **42** burgers. Burgers were sold in packs of **6**. But today burgers are on special offer with **7** burgers to a pack instead of six.

Each pack contains **7** burgers, so he buys **6** of these special packs (**6 packs × 7 burgers = 42**).

How much has he saved?

He expected to pay for seven packs and has paid for only six.

He has saved **¹/₇th** of the money he expected to pay. His calculator shows **14.3**.

Use your calculator...
1. Enter **1**
2. Press division sign (/ or ÷)
3. Enter **7**
4. Press % sign (%)

(Answer reads **14.28571**, which on rounding is **14.3%** – see *Move on with Maths: Decimals* pages 32–33 for more on rounding.)

$$\frac{1}{7} = 14.3\%$$

So the free burger is worth a discount of a seventh, or **14.3%**.

Can you do this? "Buy two, get one free!" If you really wanted three, and if they have not increased the original price, how much is this discount worth?

Give your working out on a separate piece of paper.

 Remember... Percentages are always based on an 'original amount', the amount we started with, which is given the value of **100%**.

What symbols mean

Here is a list of the common maths symbols together with an example of how they are used.

+ The symbol for adding. We say it 'plus'. In Latin plus means 'more'.

− Between two numbers this symbol means 'subtract' or 'minus'. In front of one number it means the number is a minus number. In Latin minus means 'less'.

= The symbol for equals. We say it 'equals' or 'makes'. It comes from a Latin word meaning 'level' because weighing scales are level when the amounts on each side are equal.

( ) The symbols for brackets. You do everything inside the brackets first. Brackets always occur in pairs.

× The symbol for multiplying. We say it 'multiplied by' or 'times'.

—, **/** and **÷** Three symbols for dividing. We say it 'divided by'. A pair of numbers above and below a **/** or **—** make a fraction, so $^2/_5$ or $\frac{2}{5}$ is the fraction two-fifths.

• This is a decimal point. It is a dot written after the units when a number contains parts of a unit as well as whole numbers. This is the decimal number five point six.

Index